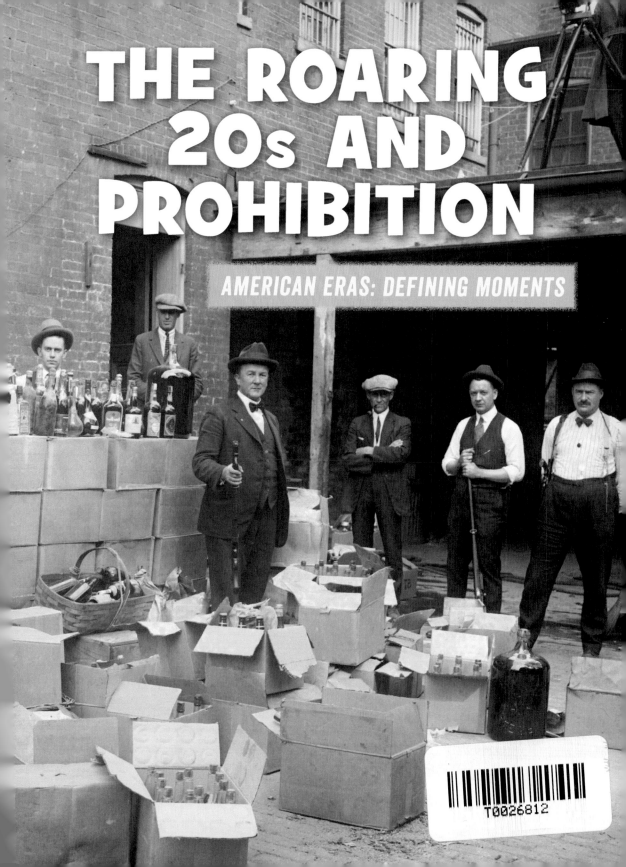

THE ROARING 20s AND PROHIBITION

AMERICAN ERAS: DEFINING MOMENTS

T0026812

CHERRY LAKE PRESS

Published in the United States of America by Cherry Lake Publishing Group
Ann Arbor, Michigan
www.cherrylakepublishing.com

Content Adviser: Kevin Whinnery, MA, History
Reading Adviser: Beth Walker Gambro, MS, Ed., Reading Consultant, Yorkville, IL
Photo Credits: © Everett Collection/Shutterstock, cover, 1; © Everett Collection/Shutterstock, 5;
  © The New York Public Library Digital Collections/Image ID 1652948, 7; © Everett Collection/
  Shutterstock, 8; © Smithsonian Institution Archives/picryl, 10; © Everett Collection/Shutterstock, 13;
  © National Archives Catalog/NA Identifier: 595674, 14; © Everett Collection/Shutterstock, 15;
  © Everett Collection/Shutterstock, 16; © Everett Collection/Shutterstock, 19; © Pamla J. Eisenberg/
  flickr, 20; © Wystan/Shutterstock, 21; © Everett Collection/Shutterstock, 23; © Everett Collection/
  Shutterstock, 24; © Everett Collection/Shutterstock, 25; © Everett Collection/Shutterstock, 26;
  © Library of Congress/LOC Control No. 93508925, 28

Copyright © 2022 by Cherry Lake Publishing Group
All rights reserved. No part of this book may be reproduced or utilized in any form or by any means
without written permission from the publisher.

Cherry Lake Press is an imprint of Cherry Lake Publishing Group.

Library of Congress Cataloging-in-Publication Data
Names: Gitlin, Marty, author.
Title: The roaring 20s and Prohibition / by Martin Gitlin.
Description: Ann Arbor, Michigan : Cherry Lake Publishing, [2021] | Series: American eras: defining
  moments | Includes bibliographical references and index.
Identifiers: LCCN 2021007863 (print) | LCCN 2021007864 (ebook) | ISBN 9781534187368 (hardcover) |
  ISBN 9781534188761 (paperback) | ISBN 9781534190160 (pdf) | ISBN 9781534191563 (ebook)
Subjects: LCSH: United States—History—1919-1933—Juvenile literature. | United States—Social life and
  customs—1918-1945—Juvenile literature. | Prohibition—United States—History—Juvenile literature.
Classification: LCC E784 .G58 2021 (print) | LCC E784 (ebook) | DDC 973.91/5—dc23
LC record available at https://lccn.loc.gov/2021007863
LC ebook record available at https://lccn.loc.gov/2021007864

Cherry Lake Publishing Group would like to acknowledge the work of the Partnership for 21st Century
Learning, a Network of Battelle for Kids. Please visit http://www.battelleforkids.org/networks/p21
for more information.

Printed in the United States of America
Corporate Graphics

ABOUT THE AUTHOR

Martin Gitlin has written more than 150 educational books. He also won more than 45 awards
during his 11-year career as a newspaper journalist. Gitlin lives in Cleveland, Ohio.

The shooting had finally stopped in Europe. World War I was over. The United States helped its **Allies** win and emerged as a stronger nation.

Americans gained confidence in their country. They believed more than ever in its ideals of freedom and **democracy**. By 1920, they were ready to enjoy the fruits of **prosperity**.

For many, this confidence meant spending and **investing** a lot of money. Many people bought things they couldn't afford to pay for immediately. They spent their earnings on expensive items like cars. They invested money in the **stock** market. They believed that the economy would continue to thrive.

Many believed the good times would last forever. It was a time of optimism and carefree lifestyles. People called it the "Roaring Twenties." Some Americans danced and **partied** without a care in the world. And they enjoyed a new form of music.

The United States experienced and recovered from a global pandemic leading up to the Roaring Twenties. America was ready for change.

The Jazz Age and Pushing the Norm

The 1920s are often referred to as the "**Jazz** Age." Playing, dancing, and listening to jazz became increasingly popular in the United States. This unique style of improvised music and dance can be traced back to African American traditions and culture. What first started in New Orleans, Louisiana, quickly grew in popularity across the nation. But the Jazz Age nickname reflected more than just the increase in the music's popularity. It also reflected the carefree outlook and lifestyle adopted by millions.

The Jazz Age promoted a fast-paced city life. Urban centers such as New York City, New York, and Chicago, Illinois, buzzed with activity. Famed writer F. Scott Fitzgerald described the time

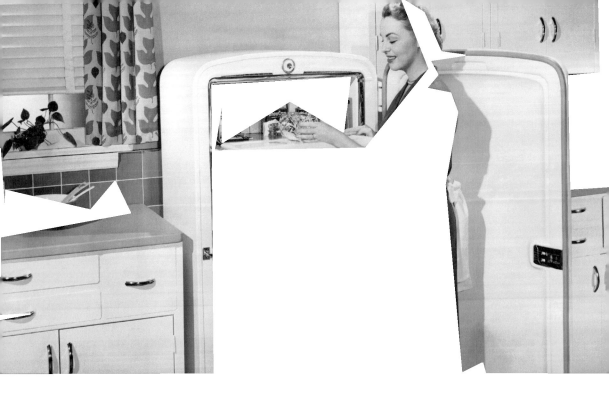

as when "the parties were bigger, the pace was faster, the buildings were higher, the morals looser."

Young people in particular embraced this new form of lifestyle and music. They often danced at parties and in night clubs to the music they loved. They took a more carefree approach to life than previous generations had.

Modern conveniences and forms of entertainment made life easier and more enjoyable. Electric washing machines and vacuum cleaners meant less time spent on housework. Elevators made living and working in tall city buildings far easier. Even using the bathroom became easier in the 1920s! Indoor flush toilets and hot and cold running water were still fairly new. People went to the movies and attended sporting events in record numbers. They listened to the radio and bought cars. Life was good.

The Great Babe Ruth

Among the celebrated figures of the Jazz Age was Babe Ruth. The New York Yankees player popularized baseball. He changed the sport forever by bringing power to the game. Ruth set many home run records. "The Bambino," as he was often called, won over fans with his outgoing personality. He was the most popular athlete in the United States in the 1920s. Read more about Babe Ruth. Why is he an important figure in history?

The Scopes Trial was also commonly referred to as the "Monkey Trial."

Many people during this era also pushed back on social norms. Among those who refused to accept traditional thinking was Tennessee high school teacher John Scopes. He dared to teach the theory of **evolution**. Before then, schools either taught **creationism** or they didn't teach the subject. Scopes's lessons violated state law.

The result was the famed Scopes Trial of 1925. It proved to be one of the most famous events of the decade. Scopes was found guilty and fined $100. But he set the foundation for the teaching of evolution in almost all American schools.

What Scopes did wasn't the only act outlawed in the 1920s. Drinking alcohol was also prohibited.

Prohibition

The date was January 16, 1920. The place was a train station in Norfolk, Virginia. The event was a funeral for John Barleycorn, led by preacher Billy Sunday.

John Barleycorn never existed. He was a fictional character from an English folk song. Barleycorn represented alcohol. Sunday was happy to "bury Barleycorn." He called alcohol "God's worst enemy."

Alcohol was indeed about to be legally dead in the United States. The U.S. Congress had voted to ban alcohol in January 1919. The new law was called the Volstead Act. It went into effect in 1920.

WHAT ALCOHOL DOES

Alcohol was believed to damage families and cloud moral judgment.

Prohibition agents, often called "Prohis," cracked down
on illegal alcohol consumption and activities.

Many people believed that alcohol was evil and needed to
be outlawed. They felt it led to bad behaviors such as laziness,
drunkenness, swearing, and crime.

Prohibition lasted 13 years. Despite banning alcohol, many
Americans found creative ways to drink illegally. Hidden bars
called speakeasies served alcohol in secret. The demand for alcohol
drove business. Daring "rumrunners" smuggled alcohol by boat
from Canada and other countries. Moonshiners made their own
whiskey and gin in **stills** while hiding from the law.

People found many ways to sneak in alcohol.

Many Americans, known as "Wets," organized protests opposing the nationwide ban. "Drys" were those in favor of Prohibition laws.

The result was a drastic increase in crime. Gangsters battled each other for business, bringing alcohol to millions. They engaged in shootouts with the police and each other. Many Americans were caught in the crosshairs and were killed. Thousands more died from poisoned homemade **liquor**. By the end of the 1920s, it was clear that Prohibition wasn't working. The law was intended to reduce violence and crime. Yet it had the opposite effect. The law was finally **repealed** in 1933.

The American economy seemed strong despite Prohibition. But it was on a shaky foundation. A collapse was looming.

The Real McCoy

One expression that gained popularity due to Prohibition was the "Real McCoy." It meant that something was real and as advertised. The expression was based on the genuine imported liquor sold by Prohibition-era rumrunner William McCoy. He gained fame among those who bought illegal alcohol. Those who sold alcohol sometimes stated that their product was "the real McCoy." What other popular expressions were born in that era? What would be today's equivalent?

A Buying Binge

Americans often took their confidence in the economy too far during the Roaring Twenties. Despite three in five Americans earning wages below the **poverty** level, many went on shopping sprees. These **consumers** were buying products they didn't need and, even worse, couldn't afford. Most of America was relying on **credit** instead of saving up money to make purchases. They were paying off expensive products, such as washing machines, cars, and radios, in monthly **installments** and **interest**. They weren't saving their money in banks. In fact, an average of four in five Americans had no savings at all. Many went into **debt**. This debt that many Americans couldn't pay contributed to the stock market crash of 1929 and led to the Great Depression of the 1930s.

[21ST CENTURY SKILLS LIBRARY]

Many businesses like department stores, gas stations, and hotels offered their best customers the ability to buy on credit.

Children go quickly and Soundly
to Sleep after a bath with ———

WRIGHT'S
COAL TAR
SOAP

7ᴰ
per TABLET
⩊
Box of
3 TABLETS
1/9

BATH
TABLETS
(double size)
1/ per TABLET
⩊
Box of
3 TABLETS
3/-

The Nursery Soap – Protects from Infection

By the end of the 1920s, over 23 million Americans were driving a car—
an item that once was only attainable by the very wealthy.

The massive purchasing of the 1920s created a false sense of prosperity. Debt forced people to live paycheck to paycheck. The loss of jobs in the 1930s, coupled with a lack of savings, prevented the American people from paying what they owed.

But not all was bad during the 1920s in America. Women finally gained the right to vote.

Big Victory for Women

For decades, American women had fought for the right to vote. They made speeches. They held rallies. They expressed their views in many forms. They pushed for an **amendment** to the U.S. Constitution as early as 1878 that would allow them to vote.

They were met with heckling and fierce resistance. Some were jailed. Others were even physically abused. But they continued to fight for their rights.

This fight was called the **suffrage** movement. Leaders such as Susan B. Anthony, Alice Paul, and Carrie Chapman Catt took part in various tactics to help their cause. Among them were pickets and even hunger strikes.

The very first Women's March was organized in 1913.

COMPUTING
DIVISION
COMPUTING
SECTION

A woman's role in society and in the home
was rapidly changing during the 1920s.

Slowly, women were being heard. By 1912, nine western states had opened the ballot box to women. In 1918, President Woodrow Wilson was vocal about his support for women's right to vote. Finally, the battle was won on August 18, 1920, when Congress ratified the 19th Amendment in a close vote.

The new law had a tremendous impact on the United States. It doubled the number of eligible voters in local, state, and national elections. Women ran for and were elected to office.

Flappers were symbolic of the new emerging freedoms of the 1920s woman.

In fact, 22 women between 1920 and 1923 ran for mayor and were elected to office in small towns across the nation, from Washington to Minnesota to Georgia.

But it took time for most American women to take full advantage of their opportunity. Only 36 percent cast ballots in the 1920 presidential election, compared to 68 percent of men.

But year after year, the number of women voters continued to rise. In 1932, they helped elect Franklin D. Roosevelt to the Oval Office. He would eventually lead the United States out of the Great Depression.

A Bit About Flappers

Among the most colorful figures of the 1920s were flappers. They were generally young, single women in northern cities who rejected conventional styles of behavior and dress. Flappers could be seen at speakeasies during Prohibition. They had short hair, wore short dresses, and tossed out their uncomfortable **corsets**. They embraced a casual and carefree lifestyle. They danced to jazz music. They were independent women. Think about the 19th Amendment and flappers. How are the two related?

Research & Act

Research some of the popular dances of the 1920s. Think about
how these dances evolved and became popular. What were their
influences? Who made these dances famous? Now, think about
a popular dance today. How do today's dances evolve and become
popular? What are their influences and who popularized them?
Discuss your research with a family member or friend. Then,
pick a dance and learn it together!

Timeline

January 10, 1920: **The Treaty of Versailles goes into effect, officially ending World War I.**

January 16, 1920: **The Volstead Act goes into effect. This law enforces the 18th Amendment banning the sale and drinking of alcohol and begins Prohibition.**

August 18, 1920: **Congress ratifies the 19th Amendment, allowing women the right to vote.**

August 2, 1923: **The death of President Warren G. Harding puts Calvin Coolidge in the White House.**

June 2, 1924: **Congress grants Native Americans full citizenship.**

July 21, 1925: **The Scopes Trial ends with a jury finding John Scopes guilty of teaching evolution. He is fined $100.**

May 20, 1927: **American pilot Charles Lindbergh leaves New York on the first nonstop trans-Atlantic flight. He lands in Paris, France, 33 hours later.**

September 30, 1927: **Babe Ruth sets a single-season record with 60 home runs.**

June 18, 1928: **Amelia Earhart becomes the first woman to complete a plane flight over the Atlantic Ocean.**

February 14, 1929: **Gangsters working for organized crime boss Al Capone kill seven rivals and citizens in the St. Valentine's Day Massacre. The murders were linked to the illegal alcohol trade brought on by Prohibition.**

October 29, 1929: **Prices of stock traded on the New York Stock Exchange crash, causing investor losses of billions of dollars. The crash ends a decade of prosperity for many and ushers in the Great Depression.**

BOOKS

Crewe, Sabrina and Scott Ingram. *The Stock Market Crash of 1929.* Milwaukee, WI: Gareth Stevens Publishing, 2005.

Kennedy, Nancy B. *Women Win the Vote: 19 for the 19th Amendment.* New York, NY: Norton Young Readers, 2020.

WEBSITES

Ducksters—U.S. History: The Roaring Twenties
https://www.ducksters.com/history/us_1900s/roaring_twenties.php

The Mob Museum—Prohibition: An Interactive History
http://prohibition.themobmuseum.org

Allies (AL-eyes) countries fighting alongside the United States in World War II

amendment (uh-MEND-muhnt) a change or addition to the U.S. Constitution

consumers (kuhn-SOO-muhrz) people who buy and use products and services

corsets (KOHR-suhts) tight-fitting, laced undergarments worn by women

creationism (kree-AY-shuh-nih-zuhm) the teaching that humans were created by God

credit (CRED-it) to buy something now but pay for it later

debt (DET) money owed to someone else

democracy (dih-MOK-ruh-see) government in which the power is held by the people, who elect their leaders

evolution (eh-vuh-LOO-shuhn) theory that humans descended from apes

installments (in-STAWL-muhnts) small, regular payments on the cost of an item bought on credit

interest (IN-trist) the money paid by a borrower for the use of borrowed money

investing (in-VEST-ing) spending money on something in the hopes of gaining more money

jazz (JAZ) American music marked by lively rhythms with unique accents

liquor (LIK-ur) a strong alcoholic beverage

poverty (POV-ur-tee) the state of being poor

Prohibition (proh-uh-BIH-shuhn) period in American history during which alcohol was illegal

prosperity (prah-SPAHR-uh-tee) a strong economic period

repealed (ri-PEELD) removed

stills (STILS) devices used to make homemade liquor

stock (STOK) a share of ownership in a company; a company has a limited number of stocks that it sells to raise money and expand

suffrage (SUHF-rij) the right to vote

INDEX